KT-594-399

THE WRECK OF THE
ARCHANGEL

GEORGE MACKAY BROWN

THE WRECK OF THE ARCHANGEL

POEMS

JOHN MURRAY
Albemarle Street, London

First published in 1989 by
John Murray (Publishers) Ltd
50 Albemarle Street
London W1X 4BD
Paperback edition 1995

© *George Mackay Brown 1989*

All rights reserved
Unauthorised duplication
contravenes applicable laws

The publisher acknowledges subsidy
from the Scottish Arts Council
towards the publication of this volume

A catalogue record for this book is
available from the British Library

ISBN 0-7195-5615 5

Typeset by Pioneer Associates Ltd, Perthshire
Printed and bound in Great Britain at
the University Press, Cambridge

To
Archie and Elizabeth Bevan

Contents

ACKNOWLEDGEMENTS

Several of the poems in this book were first published in one or
other of the *Glasgow Herald*, the *Scotsman*, the *Tablet*, and *Temenos*.

Introduction

There has been no book of poems from me since *Voyages* (1983).

That doesn't mean that I have stopped writing verse. Poetry and the making of it remains one of the great joys.

I collaborated with Gunnie Moberg in a book of photographs and poems, *Stone* (printed in a limited edition of 125 copies at the Officina Bodoni, Verona for Kulgin D. Duval and Colin Hamilton, 1987). I also worked with a group of young Scottish artists in *The Scottish Bestiary* (a limited edition of 60 books and 30 additional sets of prints, The Paragon Press, London, 1986). The best poems in those books are included here.

Several of the poems are about voyages, journeys. 'Not surprising', some readers may think; for Orkney lay athwart a great sea-way from Viking times onward, and its lore is crowded with sailors, merchants, adventurers, pilgrims, smugglers, whalers, storms and sea-changes. The shores are strewn with wrack, jetsam, occasional treasure.

Mysterious voices under the horizon have lured the young men westward always.

But this word-voyager rarely voyages far beyond his rocking-chair, and then only to take aboard a small daily cargo of errands from the shops of Hamnavoe, or drink a mug of ale.

The prospect of longer journeys – to Shetland, say, or Nova Scotia or Norway – make his cheeks blanch.

Is poetry then a fraud? Or is it a quest for 'real things' beyond the sea-glitters and shadows on the cave wall? I hope, very much, the latter.

G. M. B.
February 1989

The Wreck of the Archangel

Who saw a rudderless hulk, broken loom of cordage
That nightfall? None. In the dregs of sun
    Westraymen had drawn high the yawls.
    They fed their byred lantern-lit cows.

Indoors, women tended the different flames
Of lamp and hearth. The old ones chanted again
    Mighty tempests of foretime.
    The children tumbled gently into sleep.

Then, under the lamentation of the great sea harp,
Frailty of splintering wood, scattered cries,
    The Atlantic, full-flooded, plucking
    And pealing on the vibrant crag.

Clifftop and shore thronged soon with lanterns,
The ebb strewn with spars and with drowned
    Foreign faces, but no breached cargo,
    Wine casks or baled Baltic furs.

And all lost, all drowned, a pitiful strewment,
Emigrants set forth to root poor lives
    On a free and fruitful shore,
    Skipper and crew with seaflock scattered.

(No, but spars and planks enough to keep
An island in roofbeams, tables, coffins, doors
    A century long — a quarry of wood.
    The jaw of sea at hull gnawing all night.)

A man listens. This can't be! — One thin cry
Between wavecrash and circling wolves of wind,
    And there, in the lantern pool
    A child's face, a dwindling, in seaweed tassels,

One only glimmer. The man turns from a sure quenching.
Probe and quest in the rich ebb. A girl
    Lifts the lost cry from the sea whelm.
    It breathes, cradled, at a kindled

Hearth, a thin cold flame. He endured there
The seventy ploughtimes, creeltimes,
    Harvests of fish and corn,
    His feet in thrall always
    To the bounteous terrible harp.

Orkney: The Whale Islands

Sharp spindrift struck
At prow's turning.
Then the helmsman,
'Either whales to starboard
Or this storm
Is thrusting us at Thule,
Neighbour to bergs, beneath
The boreal star'.
Sunset. We furled ship
In a wide sea-loch.
Star-harrows
Went over our thin sleep.
Dawn. A rainbow crumbled
Over Orc, "whale islands".
Then the skipper, 'The whales
Will yield this folk
Corn and fleeces and honey'.
And the poet,
'Harp of whalebone, shake
Golden words from my mouth'.

Voyage
The Months

They have drawn and dragged a keel, down wet stones, glim of a star on one stone.

Dark water. Ropes glittered with night frost. The ship lingered, languid as snowflakes.

Wheel of wind upon waters! — the carved head snorting — plungers unseen, the crystal hooves!

They drew to a voe. Came down the jetty a girl with daffodils, wine in a jar, bread new from flames.

The sun, morning by morning, a fountain. Faces opening, flushed with northfire.

Tell us, what is the cargo? The helmsman had a stone ear.

They came to an island where dwelt, it seemed, only the young: honeycombs, harps and dances, apples. They felt their urgent witherings.

Sharp beads from the bow, cut silver swathes.

Fish, gray fruit of the shaken tree, fell into hooks, hands, the knife, the fire in the well of pinewood and stone, the purged mouths.

Sea-jarl — the hall of a sea-jarl, washings in sweet water, a fire, autumn beef and ale, welcomings, there they warmed and worded them well.

Yet now, said the skipper, *my skull is the hour glass with few grains. No oar-fold, no sail-furl, but forth-faring.*

In the deepest web of winter they wrecked on a shore. They dragged bales from the salt siege.

4

Fishermen in Winter

Such sudden storm and drifts
    We could see nothing, the boat
        Fluttering in a net
        Of reefs and crags.

The islands, blind whales
    Blundered about us. We heard
        The surge and plunge
        And the keening, all around.

Farm women had set stone lamps
    In the ledges that night.
        The village lamplighter,
        He had not thrown

Over the village his glimmering net.
    The skipper glimpsed one star
        — Soon quenched —
        But it beckoned to

A poor island with one croft.
    We moored *Fulmar*. We took
        Up to the croft door
        Two fish from the basket.

Saul Scarth
A prose poem

A man walked one morning from his croft to the well above the shore, a yoke of empty buckets at his shoulder: Saul Scarth. It was a fine summer morning. He was seen by seven people going to the well, but he did not return that day or ever to the house where an old woman waited at the hearth with a dry kettle. The flames lessened. The hearth was a cold cave at last. A star shone in the window.

THE NEIGHBOUR

I saw Saul. And I saw there was
a small boat in the Sound. Further
out, three furled masts, America-poised,
America-pointed. I saw that Saul opened
a purse, and beckoned. The man at the
tiller raised his hand. I covered my
eyes from the smuggling. They won't
drag me to the law-court in Kirkwall,
to be a witness.

THE TINKER

He'll be gone through the gray
door of the wind. He must have
drunk the moon bottle, that bright
unchancy stuff, to the last black
drop. I've gone myself a thousand
times through the silver doors of the
rain. No lowering of Saul down into the
earth door. He's unlatched the horizon,
he's in places further than Longhope or
Leith.

THE KELP BURNER

I remember thinking, 'Here he comes,
Saul.' Then I turned to the burning
tangles. I looked again. His face was
flashing above the reflections in the
well. I stirred the kelp. I saw a shape
struggling in webs of smoke.

THE MERCHANT FROM THE NEXT ISLAND

Saul S.:
2 ozs. tobacco snuff powder, 3d., for the old mother.
One pair sea stockings, 1s.
A golden love ring, one guinea.
One half sack barley seed, 2s.5½d.
(Enter in ledger, in red, 'bad debt')

SWEETHEART

I watched from the window. Then I
did not watch. We had had quarrels
the night before. I had bled his face.
That terrible temper! I'll keep my fingers
gentle as daisies. Saul, why did you not bring back
your cheek for a cure of kisses?

MOTHER

So I sat at the smoulder in the hearth
all morning waiting for water to make a
pot of tea. A man came in I didn't know.
He said, 'Mother, here I am with coins
for the herbwife, shrouder, beadle, undertaker' . . .
I had not seen that man before. He left, laughing.
The fire sank. My mouth is dry. That creature
of mine isn't back from the well yet.

THE LAIRD

Scarth gone. The whaling boats, I expect. Or
pressed for a man-o-war.
A golden hand less, next harvest. In the
snow, bowls of broth from the Hall
kitchen to that old sour mouth.

Island School

A boy leaves a small house
   Of sea light. He leaves
      The sea smells, creel
      And limpet and cod.

The boy walks between steep
   Stone houses, echoing
      Gull cries, the all-around
      Choirs of the sea,

Ship noises, shop noises, clamours
   Of bellman and milkcart.
      The boy comes at last
      To a tower with a tall desk

And a globe and a blackboard
   And a stern chalk-
      smelling lady. A bell
      Nods and summons.

A girl comes, cornlight
   In the eyes, smelling
      Of peat and cows
      And the rich midden.

Running she comes, late,
 Reeling in under the last
  Bronze brimmings. She sits
  Among twenty whispers.

Ships of Julius Agricola
Sail into the Pentland Firth

Hard rowing it was, set north. Then, six sailors
Wading ashore, flashed bronze coins
    Under a round tower
    Thick with eyes and arrows.

Was no exchange of bread or beef,
No mixing of Latin with Celtic.
    We filled six skins
    From a silver wavering stream

Under the steepest crag. We left
One coin, that the barbarians might consider
    Our *pax Romana*, petitioning soon
    For columns, laurels, law-book.

North still, the navigator muttering
Of whirlpool and whale and the winter
    Hangings of fire. There
    Beyond the utmost headland,

The helmsman called, 'whale islands'
And we saw, through gray whirls, the Orkneys.
    Then oars rose from the waves
    Heavy, as the sea had been honey

And sailors cried out, a tumult of millstones
Fell on the prow. Then, the light
    Thickening, we cast anchor
    Near the mouth of a small river.

Dawn flashed from the silver orb
Further on, where forbidden fires smouldered.
    The slaves dragged oars
    Through ash and charred skulls.

Songs for St Magnus Day

1   *The ship of Earl Magnus, going to Egilsay for a peace*
    tryst, is struck by a great wave in a calm sea

'Steer the ship into this one steep wave.
But nothing matters more.
We have brought unwanted cargo, a jar of peace' . . .
Bailing pans flashed.
The comber struck the hull, and scattered the
    oarsmen, and flawed the jar.

2   *Magnus foretells his death on Egilsay*

Sailor, your heart is a stone bowl,
The wine gone sour.
A thistle will thrust daggers through that clay
On the trysted shore.

3   *The sorrows of Magnus in the island of the church*

If your good angel stands in a door
With a song of greeting, be sure
His dark brother is biding, silent, inside.
Today a long black coat stands at the pier.
The welcomer
Folds, with his cup of keeping, at a cold fire.

4   *Magnus passes a night in the church, and a Mass is*
    said for him in the morning

So cold it is in the kirk
So dark this April night, in cell and choir
His hands dovetail
Like the one stone that locks an arch
To hold his shaken spirit still.
So cold it is, so dark.
Then, soon, the opening rose of dawn.
Calix sanguinis mei
One hand unfolds like a bird
And makes, at matin-time, a cross in the air.

5   *Magnus comes out of the church and stands among*
    his enemies

Ite: the voyage is over.
The skipper steps out of the stone ship
With a blank bill-of-lading.
A daffodil keeps a crumb of snow.
A lark
Soaks the 'isle-of-the-kirk' in a shower of lyrics.
He offers his clay to wheel and kiln once more.
Below, a ploughman
Follows, with a drift of gulls, his dithering share.

6　*The cook Lifolf is summoned by Earl Hakon to execute Earl Magnus in a stony place*

Lifolf the cook had killed a lamb
And a brace of pigeons.
A shore-stone flowered with flames.
Lifolf gave the stewpot a stir.
Eight hawk-masks stood on the hill.
'Lifolf,' they sang, 'here's better butchering —
Come up, come up!' . . .
'The lords get hungry after a hunt,' said Lifolf.
He washed his hands in the burn.
He went in a slow dance
Up to the blank stone in the barren moor.

7　*Invocation of the blind and the infirm at the tomb of Magnus*

Saint Magnus, keep for us a jar of light
Beyond sun and star.

St Magnus Day in the Island

Now the door is opened. Now the bell
    peals thrice to summon the people.
They are there, outside, a disorder of voices,
    a babble.
'Enter silently and in order.'
Came first the brothers of Peter, seven fishermen,
        with a net, smelling of strong
        salt, the silver scales in their beards.
        Seven from *Fulmar* and *Otter.*
The bell rang.
Came the miller deaf from the thunder of great stones,
        and his dusty boy.
A peal, again. (I think the island trembled from
        end to end with the joy of that bell.)
They are not long down from the hill, the shepherds,
        from dragging ewes from the blizzard, folding
        new lambs from the east wind, breaking ice
        on the stiff burn. Summer will be a golden
        time for the shepherds. (No, daffodils
        wither also.) The old shepherd leaves his
        crook at the door.
Now the bell is a trembling silence. But the boys
        have begun their psalming.

I do not know how many poor people came into the
    church. There were many humble ones, they
    kept well back, they wished to lose them-
    selves in the shadows. The boy with the
    censer threw sweetness about them.
Open, everlasting gates, sang the choristers.
All outside make way for the laird, keeper of corn
    and peathill and jetsam, lord of the longship.
    The deacon sets him not far from the very poor.
    (All are grass and flowers of grass.)
A cloud covers the sun. The window darkens. The
    candles are suddenly bright. The young
    voices go on.
Welcome to the women in their gray shawls: who most
    endure, and have the silence of stones under
    sun and rain, but cry each upon other at a
    time of tempest and grief, stone upon stone
    shaken and huddled and harshly singing and
    each more precious than onyx or ruby. They
    are given honoured place. The lady Thora
    (the mother) is among them, neither the first
    nor the last, And one a daffodil breaking
    the bud, a child. And one with ashes about
    the mouth.
Is the bishop here? William, *senex,* will enter soon
    from the vestry.
The man of iron enters, dark from forge and anvil,
    smelling of soot and burnt water, strong
    from the tolling of his black bell, and his
    boy with him bearing horse-shoes.

The master of choristers turns a page, voices flutter
like flames draught-flung. And resume,
Who is the Lord of Hosts?
Now the boatbuilders, men of the adze and nails and
the powerful keel, the caulkers, they that
curve the oars and make straight the mast,
they that send out seahorses to trample the
waves — the makers too of the little boats,
fish-seekers, that wither soon and break
upon rocks or are swallowed quick by the
Atlantic. They come, with cunning hands,
into the stone ship.
The doors must soon be closed. The doorkeeper holds
his place. Is there not room for sty-keeper
and beachcomber, the tinkers, and them that
rifle the rockpools for dulse and whelk?
There is room for all. They come in, one by one — a
knee seeks the floor, they rejoice with a
cross in the air like a shield going before
them.
Now a silence. Now there is silence, but for a jostle
and jargon outside — wherefore the doorkeeper
sets finger to mouth. The ploughmen. They
were late unyoking — the new field was stonier
than they had thought — late they were stowing
the ploughs in the lee of the barn. They come
in, one by one, the earth-workers, with the
sign of the earth: plough, and seed-sack, and
harrows, sickle and flail and winnowing fan.
The grieve from the Bu with a loaf and a
stone-jar, he is there.

Small cry of a bell at the altar.
The bishop comes in, with boys in white all about him.
    The bread and the wine are set on the altar.
Dominus pascit me, sing the boys from the hill in the
    choir.

Pilgrimage

The ship of Earl Rognvald, first of fifteen,
Gold-encrusted, left Orkney in autumn.
    Storm-beset in Biscay, they harboured
    In Spain; after Yule

Burned Godfrey's castle, and made
Twelfth Night masque with villagers.
    In a French garden the earl
    Lingered long with lyric and rose;

Endured salt of betrayal; burned
A tall-masted Moslem dromond, but lost
    Her molten gold to lobsters.
    Thorbjorn the Black, poet,

Perished in Acre, ashes after
The fever-flame, silent always under
    A sunbright howe.
    'We will come soon

To ivory and gold of Byzantium' . . .
The sailors stand now, bearing palms
    At the door of this kirk,
    The Holy Sepulchre in Jerusalem.

The Jars

A house on the mist-shrouded moor! —
the ghost of a house

Over the lintel this carving
HOUSE OF WOMEN

Not a woman stirred, outside
or in

He knocked. No-one answered.
He pushed open the door

It was dark and cold inside
the house

He opened a cupboard. In the
cupboard was a small clay
jar with markings on it

He tasted the stuff in the jar:
finest of honey! His flesh
glowed with lost suns and
blossoms. He sipped again

Now the window was black
as tar

He stooped. He stroked with
blind hands the shape of a bed.
He covered himself with coarse
weave

He slept at once

The man woke. The window
was gray. He took down the jar
to taste more honey

The single jar stood on the shelf —
the shape of it had changed, and it
was of coarser clay

He opened it. It was crammed
with salt.

(The man heard, somewhere in
the house, a small cry)

He went through the rooms
of the house in search of a
child. The house was empty still

He returned to the room with
the cupboard and jar. He said,
*Young one, whoever you are, you
won't starve because of me —
There will be fish for the salting*

He came to a room where
the hearth was cold and the
lamp empty

On a stone of the wall was
carved the shape of a fish

He looked at the rune so long
that it seemed to pass into him
and become part of him

In another room, hidden, a
girl was singing

The man said, *Lost and
darkling creature, I will bring
you oil and driftwood
always*

The song guttered out. It
stopped. It faltered into
low cries of pain

The man wandered again
through the rooms of the house

He saw his reflection in a
pane. Furrows in the face,
a mesh of gray through his
black beard

A poor house, he said.
There should be a bowl
on the sill, daffodils
or roses or heather, to say
what time of year it is — yes —
to spill some beauty into a
bleak place. This jar is all,
it seems

He took the jar from the shelf.
An earth smell came out of it —
it was half full of flailed corn.
His hands that held the jar were
twisted with a summer of pain

Through the corridors of the
house a contented cry came. It
must (he thought) be a woman over
new loaves and ale, well pleased,
arms and face fire-flushed

Lost one in this house, he
said, *there will always be*
cornstalks — I will see to it

He scratched an ear-of-corn
on a stone beside the stone
with the carved fish

He lay down on the bed.
He was as weary as if he
had toiled, sunrise to
sunset, in a harvest field

He lay under a green and
a gold wave

His dream was about the
one jar that flowed always
from shape to shape, and
was ripeness, keeping, care,
sorrow, delight

The man woke. He knew now
that he was old

A thin-spun silver flowed over
the blanket. His hands were like
shreds of net, or winter roots

Seven women of different
ages stood about his bed. They
all, from first to last, had the
same fleeting look: the lost
girl at the horse fair

One by one, beginning with
the youngest, they bent over
and kissed him

The mid-most woman smelt
of roses and sunlight. Her
mouth had the wild honey
taste

The oldest one dropped
tears on his face

Then the seven women
covered their faces and
went out of the room

He slept on into the starred
ebb of winter

He opened his eyes

A young man was
standing in the open door. He
carried a jar on his
shoulder

The young man greeted
him — then he turned
and went out into the
sun

The man said, *That is
my son. He is carrying
away the dust of my
death*

Poems for Kenna

1 THE PRINCE IN THE HEATHER

'He is safe in Paris.
He circles among high-spoken ladies.
Long fingers touch the harpsichord.'

'No. I saw him last week
On the flank of Schiehallion
Laughing
Up near the snowline, with laughing friends.'

'There was no such prince.
The mountain people
Dreamed for half a century, then woke among ruins.'

'How can a young man delicately bred
Eat coarse bannocks
And lie at night under rain and stars?
The terror, wakening, of gold and betrayal!'

'I was on that shore, hidden,
When the foreign ship let down a rope
Into his tinker-dark hands.'

'Because of that Stuart
I stand useless with one arm
At the nets
Or when the harvesters heave through their golden sea.'

'No dream, no disgrace.
I was with Charlie
When we broke the lock of the tower,
But drowned soon
In Saxon blood and steel, on the stone stair.'

'She that we stormed the fortress for,
Alba,
She will be a crone from this day forward,
Her lovely Gaelic
Lost in whiskers and toothlessness.'

So I, bard at Strathnaver, heard
From poet after poet
In deserted chapel and hall, and in fireless huts
All down the glens, that summer,
Going on to a strange shore, summoned.
Battles, betrayals, dynasties.
What salves for their ancient pain?
The swords and the harps lay broken.
'I have word of a well of loveliness in the west.
Its overspillings
Will brighten our mouths for the new music.'

My silver coin flashed in the sun.
The boatman at the rock
Shook the gull from the rowlock.
   — 'I will ferry you to Coll, man.'

2   *SAILING TO PAPAY*

Prow set for Greenland, a westerly
Weeks-long, a graybeard gale
    Drove *Skarf* at Iceland,
    A bleak shore, behind it

A burning mountain. One farm all night
Thrummed with harpsong and saga
    But a hard mouth at dawn
    Bargained for cheese and eggs.

The gale northerly then, a hag
Spitting hail, herded *Skarf*
    Among Faroese yoles, rowlock-deep
    In drifts of salmon.

Cold we challenged across the Sound,
Banter with bargaining, the Faroemen
    Squeezed one silver coin
    From our hoard, for seven sea-heroes.

'Now,' said the skipper, 'you won't be seeing
The Greenland girls, nor yet gathering
    Vinland grapes. Fate
    Flings our keel at Shetland.'

Fame-lust, beyond glebe or gold,
Had launched us on that ocean
    Not to be arguing at sunset
    The price of a barrel

Of sour ale, and smoked mutton, with
A surge of Shetland women on a shore.
    We held south, we ran past
    Islands thin as plates.

On the Island of the Celtic Priests
Beyond, I at the helm saw
    On a seal-flecked shore
    A girl of such brightness

The king's tax-hoard in a Bergen vault
Held not such a torrent of gold.
    The twenty young oarsmen
    Followed my cry and flung finger.

3 A WRITER'S DAY

Gulls

It was a long day in his field
Turning furrows like pages.
He strove towards a sign, the cornstalk.

The Inn

At noon he went to the inn.
Voices, smoke, shadows. He sifted
One heavy hard gleam from the gossip.

Fisherman

A fisherman came in, gale tangled,
With a basket of haddocks.
He struck a fish-shape in the stone of his mind.

Child

He met a child from the school, dawdling.
The wind
Strung gold across her quiet face.

Gravedigger

In the kirkyard, a spade
Knocked on the earth door.
In a croft, on the far side of the hill, a long silence waited.

Sunset

His seaward window smouldered, black and red.
Would a poem come with the first star?
Lamplight fell on two white pages.

Stranger
The latch lifted. A stranger came in
So beautiful
She seemed to be a woman from the sea.

4   *A CAROL FOR KENNA*

Many a wanderer this day-wane walks
A winter world; with luck
    Under first stars, might find
    A hovel (the hearth long black,

A crack through the stone cupboard.) That one
Will have the raftered owl for room-mate,
    A cat's shadow shifting
    Along the garden ruckle

That once kept kale, tatties,
Fuchsia, rosebush, butterflies,
    Bees, echoes of laughter,
    Lost children, all gone

Into the last darkness and silence,
Intensities deeper than snow.
    Listen. New stones
    Are being quarried and set

This very day for love and birth
And for laughter and welcoming
    Round an unmade hearth-fire.
    This sunset, near the solstice,

Lost a little between two images
I offer praise in a winter poem
    For a very dear friend
    Who has come from Pacific suns
    To sit, a guest, at my fire.

Interrogation

How was the journey, man?
Darkness. A trudge in sun and wind and rain. Now,
$\qquad\qquad\qquad$ again, shadows.

What holds the line that curves upon itself, end to
$\qquad$ *beginning? Can you tell?*
A grave centre.

Lissomness stoops to dust. Plough and fiddle are
$\qquad$ *dust. Children are tall distant dust. Love is*
$\qquad$ *dust of roses. Vanitas, grainings.*
I honour the jar and the grains in the round jar.

Here's your door. Wait. Listen. Silence deeper than snow.
I accept the solstice.

What then, afterwards?
No more. The circle is closed.

The dance of clay goes on. You are not a memory any
$\qquad$ *more among your waters and cornfields and skies.*
$\qquad$ *What then?*
The millstone is quiet; then turns.

You are lost, man, among the atoms and planets.
I am content to be here beside a broken kirk
$\qquad\qquad$ where the poor have been fed.

The House
Stations of the Cross

In such granite rock
How shall a house be built? Let them see to it.

After the rains, men dug to the hard rock.
The carpenter strove with the roof-tree.

A scaffolding fell.
Three drunk labourers were given their books.

She who was to grace the finished house,
Baker of the loaves, keeper of the loom,
She stood in a web of rafters.

The work languished. Another mason was sent for,
A man of solid reputation.

One hot day a girl took a jar of ale to the site.

Thunder in August wrenched an iron lattice,
A sudden brilliance out of the banked gray and purple.

Masons laid a lintel, a long cold stone.
Women stood here and there.
They gossiped. They nodded. They said, 'house of sorrow'.

Before harvest labourers climbed down from the eaves.

A diviner went in a slow dance.
Earth was struck into tumults of bright
                                circles.

Dazzle — first snow — on planed and sanded pine.
At the time of crocuses
Carpenters put the last nail in the staircase.

Painters, tilers, men with snibs and latches —
Ladders and planks and buckets borne away.
The architect's voice from the balcony, 'It is
                                finished.'

The woman came again with daffodils.
She set a jar on the sill.

And still the house echoed like a tomb
Till the village women arrived with gifts.
They stayed to eat the cakes from the new-lit
                                hearth.

From The Scottish Bestiary

MOTH

The moth travels from pane to pane, in August
Wherever a lamp is set.

There's old Sammy playing his fiddle,
Such a rant
The sweet plea of the moth at the pane is lost.

In the next croft
Three children are reading their school books.
He thuds on the pane.
They are lost in labyrinths: seaports, poetry, algebra.

Travel on, moth.
The wife is out in the byre, milking.
A fire-drowsed dog
Growls at the birring in the window.

Will nobody help a lost moth?
All he wants
Is a rag to chew, best of all
The golden rag in the lamp.

The moon is too far away.

In the next three crofts:
Ploughmen were drinking ale from a cog
And an old woman was knitting a sock
And a twisted couple
Were counting pieces of silver out of a sock
On to a scrubbed table.
They looked scared at the moth's delicate knock.

Ah, the fisherman is mending a creel in his shed
In a circle of light.
The moth enters on a sea-draught.
Ecstacy of flame
Hurls him to the floor, scorched.
And the fisherman says,
'Night-fly,
I wish the skate were as keen to come on my hook.'

The moth woke to ashes, dawn, a cold lamp.

LOBSTER

What are you doing here
Samurai
In the west, in the sunset streams of the west?

How you lord it over those peasants,
The whelks
The mussels and the shrimps and scallops.

There you clank, in dark blue armour
Along the ocean floor,
With the shadows flowing over you,
Haddock, mackerel,
And the sun the shadow of a big yellow whale.

Nothing stands in your way, swashbuckler.

The orchards where you wander
Drop sufficient plunder,
Mercenary in the dark blue coat of mail.

Be content, be content far out
With the tides' bounty,
Going from smithy to smithy, in your season
For an ampler riveting.

Fold your big thumbs,
Under the trembling silver-blue scales of the moon.

RAVEN

Nothing still: the west empty.
The sail useless in this north-westerly.
Sea too rough for the oars.
The raven in the wicker cage, he rages more than the seamen.

The seamen have their cheese and beer.
(For the raven, no food.
That raven hated us, through his bars).
Sun went down, russet.
'A good sign,' said the skipper,
But like all of us could hardly speak
For the shaking of his teeth.
We were cold men, from spindrift and hail showers.
A few stars came out
And they had the faces of children.
The young seamen slept.
I lay cold all night. The raven did not sleep.
The helmsman did not sleep.
Yet there is land in the west: Orcades, Alba, Ireland.
Raven screamed with hunger at dawn.
He screamed, seeing our oatcakes and beer.
Then sudden the wind swung nor-east,
The sail drank the nor-east
And *Seeker* went like a stallion over the gray field
                              of the sea white-flowered.
He whose mouth was full of dooms
Pictured us galloping
Over the roaring edge of the world.
The young sailors, cheerful with the wind,
Laughed, and wind laughed,
And laughter of sea lay all about us.
(The starved raven, he laughed not.)
'Now let the raven go free.'
The boy unlatched the raven's cage
Cautiously, lest the raven have his eye.

But no, all thin as he was,
The raven leapt at the sun, and wheeled
High, and higher, and flung
His hollow eye round the horizon's ring,
And fluttered no bigger than a fly
Westward. Like a black arrow
The raven sped then into the empty west.
Then was our skipper glad.
Then he flung his arm about this shoulder and
                                        that.
'There is land there.
Our friend Raven has smelt worms and carrion.
Raven will be there first.
Seamen, keep your axes well honed.
There is land for us in the west,
Islands, fertile straths, mountains for goat pasture,
Fiords full of fish.
Boy, you shall have a sweetheart in Alba.'
One day still we followed the raven.
Then the helmsman pointed to a hill.

WHALE

He has broken his boreal bounds, the whale.
Sea seethes about him
Like cauldron on cauldron of ale!

The rinsed eye of the whale
Sees, through spindrift and smother
A watchful wind-drinking sail.

A snow-cloud lours on the whale.
The armoured hide
Rebounds with volleys of sleet and ice and hail.

He pastures deep down, the whale.
The dreaming plankton,
Over his delicate lip they drift and spill.

He must breathe bright air, the whale.
He surges up,
A sudden fountain flowers from his skull.

What bothers him now, the whale?
A boat-ful of men.
He scatters them with a lazy sweep of the tail.

A harpoon has struck the whale.
And the barb quickens.
The iron enters him slowly, cell by cell.

Go to the lee of the berg, wounded whale!
He welters in blood.
The eye dims, and the foundry heart is still.

EAGLE
The Child Stolen from the Harvest-field

An eagle, circling high.
The swaddled child
Lay in the bronze
Shadow of a barley stook.
The mother,
Bronze-throated, bent and gathered and bound.
The eagle
Hovered, stooped, threshed.
The child hung
Hooked in talons, dragged
Up blue steps of sky
To a burning nest
In a crag of Coolag hill.

The harvest mother
Followed. She changed
Burnish for blue wind,
Bleeding hands. She
Lifted the boy like an egg
From the broken
Circles of beak and claw and scream.
She brought him down
To her nest of crib and milk.
She kissed him.
She lit the lamp.
She rocked the cradle. She sang.

Old grand-da muttered
Through the gray
Spittle and smoke of his pipe,
'Better for the boy, maybe
That freedom of rock and cloud,
A guest
In the house of the king of birds —
Not what must come,
Ten thousand brutish days
Yoked with clay and sea-slime.'

Henry Moore:
Woman Seated in the Underground

How many thousands of years she has travelled
To come to this place.

Above, burning wind
Broken stone and water.

She has sat in Troy and Carthage and Warsaw.
She has endured ice and sun.
She sits, pure from those weatherings.

Is she waiting for the hunters and soldiers to come home?

Does she hear
The laughter of lost children?

She breaks the long vigil
With spinning, baking, gossip, welcomes and farewells. In April
she will set daffodils in a jar.

Fires, shaking of cornerstones!
Nineteen-forty. This is her longest winter.

London is burning and breaking above her.
Persephone, wait on your throne.

The Old Actor in Athens

I masqued kings and wore a tinsel crown.
Next play, I was the cunning one
Who scrawled the plan of a labyrinth on a skin
And laid stone upon stone
And prisoned there a thing half-beast, half-man,
Till the hero came with the skein.
I was Achilles above a streaming mane
And thunder of hooves on the plain
When Hector, maggot-blown,
Hither and thither, this way and that, was thrown,
Great Priam's son.
The Trojan walls were thronged with the soon-to-be-slain.
Scullion and spinner and queen
Wove from mouth to mouth the ancient keen.
The lips of Helen made a thin cold line.
Orpheus I was, the hell gate clashing behind, alone
In the wind and the rain,
Alone, after the music, with his pain.
(The crowd throws gold and flowers. The masker grows vain.)
Another masque. A ship cleaves the main,
Old sailors young with salt and boasting and wine,
Ulysses I, we lean,
Discoverers yet, into a sea unknown,
Out to the cold gray streams where the sun goes down.
And I was the king that pierced his eyes with a pin.
(Gray in the beard. The voice gets cracked and thin.
For masker and dancer soon

Only a random handclap, a silver coin.
Yes, but our mimes, every now and again
Distil to one
Pure lucent drop of benison
The fogs that rot the heart with each breath drawn
Until men seal the urn;
They honour the seven coats about the bone.)
At last I was one in a rabble, some street scene,
A drunken clown.
They put on me the mask of a keeper of swine.
The manager said, 'If you want to stay on,
Sweep up the empty grape-skins with broom and pan
When the curtain's down
And the crowd goes off to the wine shops in the town' . . .
So, a dog's day is done
Who once was Midas on a golden throne.

'Throw a mite to the old mimic-man'.

John Barleycorn

I stirred in a cell deep underground
Blind, no taste or smell, no touch, no sound.

One day I slid the bar from the door.
I poked a pale nose into the air.

What was to be seen?
My hair and hands in the sun were green.

I saluted a canty old creature —
Mister Scarecrow, a stick and a tatter.

I was very poor, but then
I could dance to the pipe of the wind, the
                              thrummings of rain.

The lark with its fluttering sky-weary breast
Was often my guest.

One morning I brightly awoke —
I was wearing a prince's yellow cloak!

I thought my dancing days would never be done
Under the sun.

A mud-coloured knave with a crooked knife
Stood before me, he threatened my life.

He severed me from my root.
He bound me hand and foot.

He beat the flesh from my bones.
In a double circle he trapped me, thundering stones.

O bitter hurt,
The graining and ooze of the heart!

'Can you sink, John, can you float?'
He scattered my dust in a seething vat.

The torturer
Finished his work with the red sign of fire.

In furrows born,
Forever I flush the winters of men with wassails of corn.

Greenpeace

The small kings bargain and feud and fight.
Among them, unhindered
Pass the wandering priest and the bard.
I seek, I sing the goodness of this land, said the poet,
More lovely to me than a sweetheart.
The Kings of Pictland
Gave passage to his harp up the broken waters of the west —
How, being briefly troubled, it returns to purity,
Always the blood and the rust
Are washed by sea and mist and rains.
The kind mother
Cleanses her children from cornsweats and slime of fish . . .
Therefore this bard
Left the beautiful village of Glasgow.
He passed the Inversnaid torrent,
And he lingered at a beach in Barra,
And at Iona knelt awhile
For the purifying of his harp with meditation and psalms.
In winter, among the mountains,
The harp rejoiced in the whiteness and coldness of snow.
He sat, one week of westerly gale
At fishermen's fires.
He gave them a song for Minch herring, a cluster, a soundless
                                                silver bell.

Northwards, in Orkney, men piled
A longship with arrows and axes
For venturing (but it was murder, burning, pillage

As far as Man and Scilly.)
The seamen stopped their lading. Poets are welcome,
They remind men of the great circle of silence
Where the saga sails forever.

A peaceful ship gave him passage
Through the Pentland Firth, the bow
Thrusting the strenuous waters this way and that.
He saw under a Caithness crag
A fisherman hanging salmon nets to take, at dawn,
Glitterings of sun and wind.
Later, at a market, at Dee-mouth,
Silver of mackerel exchanged for silver mintings.
There, among barrels,
Hungerer struck harp, a fish was given.

What bard now to strike
The rock of elegy
For sea, the lost mother?
(The harp is flown,
Carved ship-with-mariners
A museum stone.)
Skua, whale, herring
Litter a rotted shoreline.

Cover mouth till the bell is struck.

Our veins run still
With salt and questing of ocean,
Eyes to unlock horizon,
New lucencies, new landfalls.
Poets of machine and atom,
A last bird at a tidemark
Announces the death of the sea.

Follow the harp, songless one.
Find the bride
Asleep, in lost Atlantis, beside the fountains of waters.

Desert Sleepers

Dawn opened, a rose
Upon three travellers asleep.

The moon
Drifted from them, a worn
Washed shell.
             They slept.

The well
Beside the palm, a deep
Pearl glimmer.

They had come far.
They slept out
The seven flashing mirrors of the sun.

One woke. Twilight
Silently
Battered a bronze nail (a star)
In the west.

The dreamers awoke. A new wind
Lifted
The red petals from their eyes.

Rackwick: A Child's Scrapbook

The valley was a green jar,
    corn crammed

The green bowl
    brimmed with milk, honey, fish-oil

Once, the green jar
    tilted at sixteen hungry doors

Sealed in the jar now
    dust of old laughter and grief

They say, the jar flawed
    with heaviness of coins

Long fallen, the jar — shards
    half hidden in rushes

Hills tell old stories. Cliffs
    are poets with harps

Brightnesses broached —
    Shoal, peatbog, sheaves

Waver west, fish, with moon and stars.
    The sun's a cornstalk

'Every day,' says the sea,
    'I count shell and wrack'

Stone in the burn
    counts millions of urgent waterdrops

The burn numbers
    roots, clouds, trout

'In my pocket,' says the cloud,
    'a thousand silver coins'

The rose
    spills incense and cold curls, a candle

Worm shares with lark
    charlock, broken gold

'Soon now,' sang the peat,
    'I'll wear a red and yellow dress'

Welcome, eagle. That bird
    is home after a hundred years

Buttercup, iris, clover
　　idle in troops at the sun's door

Cornstalk cries, 'I'm the heir,
　　first child of the sun-king!'

The shy worm, 'I toil
　　in a cellar of the king's castle'

Thugs are abroad with knives in July
　　— clegs!

Yes, bandits too with rows of knives in their mouths
　　— rats!

Midges in millions, at sundown, tapping
　　cellars of blood

Mouse, clever thief
　　unlocking stone to get to butter and candles

'No rose this,' sang
　　the bee on the rusted barb

Has a lark
　　slept in a bed of nettles, ever?

I wonder, does the butterfly
    say *hullo* to the spider?

Listen — *plop!* — a trout
    has been gossiping with a cornstalk

Oh, bee
    to die in the heart of that rose. . .

The Island of the Children

A man with a silver beard wrote an invitation
To a boy or a girl from every country on earth
To a picnic on his island.
They came, one after the other, one morning.
They were all delighted with the black boy
Because he was black as ebony,
And with the Chinese girl
Because she was yellow as starlight
And with the Eskimo boy
Because he was plump and smelt of ice and whales
And with the Greek girl
Because she was honey-coloured
And her words and her breath were like honey too.
The Arab boy
Ran through the fields with the Jewish girl
And their voices mingling
Were like one ancient wise harp of praise.
A girl from Siberia and a boy from Arizona
Had great wonderment
Describing 'bear' and 'cactus' to one another.
The hundred and fifty children
Delighted in all the animals round them
And the fish and the birds and insects.

It seemed that day would never end
Till the old enchanter
Who had lured them to his island
Sang, 'The sun's down!
Time to go home, to get on in the world and
be wise' . . .

The hundred and fifty children
Woke up in scattered beds.
A long long time had passed.
They found themselves the rulers of their countries,
White-haired, grave, and honoured.
They made important speeches
About 'freedom', 'progress', and 'peace'.
From time to time they spoke to each other
Across long distances, coldly.
They set spies to spy on all the others.
They had maps with shifting frontiers.
They revolved those globes often.
At last a silver-haired President
Discovered the Island of the Children on his map.
His heart sang like a lark that dawn.
But it was too late.
A thousand missiles were hurtling here and there.

The Black Horseman

'L ook out, he's coming.
The black horseman is coming!'
Children run down from the hill,
Wild flowers spill
From their hair and hands.
Down the net-spread sands
The fishermen push out errandless boats.
Only the goats
Are content on the hill, and the cows
Shift their slow jaws.
Ploughman the furrow has fled, shepherd the fold.
The laird double-locks his chest of plate and gold.
He's off to his town abode
Quicker than lover or highwayman ever rode,
His wife up behind.
They pass dunghill and dump like scented wind.
Doors are barred, windows shuttered.
'What's all the fuss?' one old man muttered.
'To a gray fire-sider
He's a good friend, that jet-black rider.
Sooner he comes, the better.'
Girls at the bench of cheese and butter
In the great farm
Run here and there in whirls of alarm,
Apple-bright girls
Driven by a shadow to shrieks and skirls.

The calm birds angle and circle and go.
The jaunty scarecrow
Cares not a jot
For the whirling hoof of the stallion of jet.
The preaching man droops here and there,
All DOOM and BEWARE.
A tinker boy
Sprawls in a ditch to see the black horseman go by.
'The black horseman is coming!'
Stones of the hidden hamlet echo the hooves' drumming.
The sun goes dark.
It falters and falls from the blue, the light-drained
                                                    lark.

The Horse Fair

Miss Instone said, 'Children, you were all at the Fair
yesterday, I'm sure. Out slates! Out slate pencils! Write a
composition on the following — My Day at the Fair. . . '

Twelve slate pencils squeaked and squealed on slate like mice in a
barn.

Willie rubbed honey-of-sleep out of his eyes. He wrote.

I went to the Horse Fair.
I sat in the cart beside old Da.
In Dounby
We left Daffodil in the Smithfield yard.
A policeman was holding on to a man that could hardly stand.
Old Da gave me a penny and a farthing.
Old Da went into the inn.
I bought a bottle of stone ginger at an old wife's tent.
I saw hundreds and hundreds of people.
I saw Skatehorn the tramp.
Mr Sweyn went on with a long stick and a deer-stalker
And the women curtsied in his wake.
I saw Old Da in the crowd at last,
His face was like a barn lantern.
We stood and watched the tug-o'-war.
What red faces, bulging eyes, what staggerings!

It came on to wind and rain.
The whisky tent
Blew out like a ship in a gale.
Old Da had dealings with the blacksmith,
Nails and a new plough.
The blacksmith wrote numbers and words in a ledger, after he
                              had licked a small blunt pencil.
The blacksmith
Took a bottle and two glasses from a stone shelf.
He gave me sixpence!
We went home in the cart, Daffodil
Danced all the way.
She struck many stars from a stone.
The fiddler! — I nearly forgot the fiddler.
The whole Fair
Seemed to go round his fiddle. I saw
A coal-black man stretched on a board of nails.
Three farmers,
Quoys and Graygarth and Longbreck,
Seemed like they had red patches sewn on their faces, coming out
                              of the whisky tent.

Daffodil
Whinnied at the stars, 'What are you,
Nails or mayflowers?'
The moon was a skull.
Then the moon was bees and honey.
I woke up.
Old Da carried me out of the cart to our fire.

'Spelling and punctuation need special attention,' said Miss Instone. 'Few of you, it seems, had a really enjoyable day.'

Sprinkling of water on eleven slates, rag rubbings, sighs.

Willie spat on his slate and wiped out that day with the sleeve of his gray jersey.

From Stone

FLOWER OF THE STONE

Flower of the stone,
  Fire on a hearth.

Flower of the stone,
  A jar of honey.

Flower of the stone,
  A jar of oats.

Flower of the stone,
  Fulmar, unfurling.

Flower of the stone,
  Butterfly, thistledown, bee.

Flower of the stone,
  A name, two dates, cut deep.

The tall shore dust,
  Fish seekers, drift
    Among the heavy flowers.

SEASCAPE:
THE CAMERA AT THE SHORE

In the rockpool a child dips (shrilling)
Fingers, toes.

Below the widest ebb it opens,
The lost sea rose.

Then, drowning rose and reef and rockpool
The west inflows. . .

The Atlantic pulse beats twice a day
In cold gray throes.

Shy in a rock-caught crumb of earth
One seapink shows.

Scotland, scattered saw-teeth, melts like petals
In the thin haze.

Lucent as a prism for days, this shore, until
A westerly blows.

Then stones slither and shift, they rattle and cry,
They break and bruise.

Shells are scattered. Caves like organs peal
Threnody, praise.

Tangles lie heaped in thousands, thrust and thrown
From the thunder and blaze!

Silence again. Along the tidemark wavelets
Work thin white lace.

Among that hoard and squander, with her lens
Gunnie goes.

FOREIGN SKIPPER: 17TH CENTURY

Tell us then, skipper, about the islands. Were there people?
　　Men with Ploughs and Boats
　　　　(fruitful curving Wood), Women
　　　　with Fire and Water, Children,
　　　　Giants in a stone circle.

Were there trees?
　　No trees. Wind cut too sharp from
　　　　North and east. There were Stones.

Cities?
　　The smallest City, a stone cluster,
　　　　at the heart of the city a stone
　　　　Kirk. The Kirk seemed a Ship.
　　　　Earth-rooted, it sought (red) the
　　　　Gold of sunrise

Were there fruits?
  Little black Globes in coarse
    stone-scattered Grass that
    stained the Mouth.

Animals?
  Horses, Whales, Oxen, Goats,
    Swine, Bees, Eagles, Fish.

Were there dragons? Did you hear the music of that folk?
  Fiddles. I saw a Dragon carved on
    a stone.

Were there stones?
  Everywhere, like Flowers. Stones
    of great beauty, Wave-blown.

STONE AND STAR

  The stone that sinks a creel
  The stone that whets a scythe
  The stone
  That locks a bridge over the burn
  The stone that keeps milk cold
  The ordered stones that stand between hearth
                            and a winter storm
  The carved stone over the nest of skulls
  The stone that children
  Enchant to flower, ship, castle

The stone sea-vested twice a day
The stone the beachcomber
Strikes a match on to light his pipe
Between a crag and a stormfall,
A tall stone in a field
Strayed reveller from the circling Brodgar dance,
The seapink stone
The stone the Ice Giant dragged out of Norway
The stone, Hesper,
That kisses a darkling ebbtide stone.

SHORE SONGS

The crab said, 'I'm locked in this pool
Until the Atlantic
Rolls back, and turns the blue key.'

The seapink said, 'I stand awhile
On a bare rock.
All summer I breathe salt and sun, then I die.'

The shell
To the child's shell-cold ear gives back
The innumerable choirs of the sea.

A driven ship in a gale,
A reef, a wreck.
'Here I lie, a piece of that kiss ever since,'
                the stone sang secretly.

BUILDING THE CROFT HOUSE

We took the first basket
Near the Old Man,
We climbed, loaded. We crossed Moorfea.
We set down the stones.

This we did, we two
A hundred days
Between boat launch and butter making.

Peat-cutting, stone-getting, stone-dressing, stone-setting.
That summer
A dream of stone, fish, corn.

We carried up stones
In June, when the grass was tall and bee-thronged.
A gable looked out over the bay.

Flashing scythes, falling corn.
The doorstep set.
We drank ale from a stone jar.

Hearth-stone, water niche, lintel.
Small stones sang from the chiselled querns.
I can't work wood.
I had to give silver for roof-beams, door, table.

We carried the last load
Two days before the wedding.

The day after the first snow
Sam the ox stood in the byre. He chewed. He wondered.

TIME A STONE

Storm and sea loss and sorrow is all
An old mouth at a rock

Tomorrow's wave will cover that boy and his yawl
An old mouth at a rock

Trust only the sweet clean water in the well
An old mouth at a rock

Let other girls wake to the black sea yell
An old mouth at a rock

Once I was lissom and sweet and tall
An old mouth at a rock

Fishermen hung sea silver at my wall
An old mouth at a rock

One lingered, fishless. My blood beat like a bell
An old mouth at a rock

I lit a lamp at a secret sill
An old mouth at a rock

A kiss is a cruel spell
An old mouth at a rock

A summer of kisses, then all goes ill
An old mouth at a rock

On the rosetree scents and petals sicken, they fall
An old mouth at a rock

Strength and goodness go under the hill
An old mouth at a rock

No songs but from the mouth of a child or a shell
An old mouth at a rock

And time a stone, and the feet of the dancers still
An old mouth at a rock

THE MASQUE

Cometh one in a green coat, he follows broken earth.
Rainbow coats follow, children. They dance in sun and pools.
Cometh a blue coat with a fish sewn on it.
Cometh a gray one, a spinner.

She labours
To cover a thing brighter than sun
Till the dust of seventy summers
Devours weft and stitch. . . Silence again: brightness, a bone.
Cometh the one in black, with a black flute.
All dance together.
The one in a green coat
Makes the sign of breaking, of beckoning, then of peace.
The masque
Was before dust or harp. It moved
With the first movement of stone and water.

A STONE CALENDAR

JANUARY
> The icy stone —
> a fortress in Siberia

FEBRUARY
> Hall of prisms:
> rain, haar, spindrift

MARCH
> Silence: a stone cell.
> Around,
> Shell choirs, abrim

APRIL

The sun temple, two lochs,
   dance of sixty stones

MAY

The stone: brief
   Inn of a butterfly.

JUNE

Sea-pink, fish-girl,
   a vigil at a sea wall

JULY

Bee blunders from stone to flower,
   heavy, harping
   to the golden city

AUGUST

Whetstone, quern, kiln —
   three harvest stones

SEPTEMBER

One small shadow
   drifts to the door of the stone

OCTOBER

A star hangs, a lantern
   at the stone's lintel

NOVEMBER

A host of shadows
clusters
about the House-of-the-Dead

DECEMBER

Silver key, snowflake, star-wrought.
Three sea kings
seek the House-of-Bread.

MILE STONE

How many miles to the kirk of Magnus?
Fifteen

And to the circle of Brodgar stones?
Four

And to the sea valley in Hoy?
Six,
As the seagull flies

And to the village where the Irish soldier
Built his inn? . . . Seven

How many miles to that other place, the Inn of Night?
Ask a blank stone in the kirkyard

The mile stone
Has opened a wise mouth a many a year
To horseman and traveller

How many miles to the lost children?
The stone
Cries in a daffodil surge, with spindrift of dew

SONG OF THE STONE

Said stone to buttercup,
'Dance till you're yellow rags, then die.'

Said stone to seagull,
'A broken egg, a chalky skull in a niche of a crag,
Not long, not long.'

The stone spoke to the man going with a plough.
'A mouthful of bread and ale,
Then the long sleep, under snow.'

Sang stone to star,
'Burn, cold candle. I wear after rain the swarming colours of day.'

Said stone to raindrop,
'Don't run.
We're for the mill, you and I, to grind bread.'

Stone in hourglass
Whirls, sighs, sinks upon silence.

In Memoriam I. K.

That one should leave The Green Wood suddenly
  In the good comrade-time of youth,
  And clothed in the first coat of truth
Set out alone on an uncharted sea:

Who'll ever know what star
  Summoned him, what mysterious shell
  Locked in his ear that music and that spell,
And what grave ship was waiting for him there?

The greenwood empties soon of leaf and song.
  Truth turns to pain. Our coats grow sere.
  Barren the comings and goings on this shore.
He anchors off The Island of the Young.

The Silent Girl from Shetland
A prose poem

At the year's beginning I too made a beginning, to pilgrim to Orkney.

But I am a poor man that has no boat of my own. But I have a hardworking wife that spins wool and knits beautiful things.

And we have a poor dumb girl.

There was much storm that month.

The wool my wife spun in February looked gray in the white dazzlement of snow coming in at our open door.

And I took my score of sheep into shelter but two died in the blizzard.

The dumb girl wept without sound about the bright graves of the two sheep, in February.

In March, in the village of Scalloway, my wife got a shilling for the scarves and stockings she had knitted.

How the wind blew in mid-March! Fishing boats were hauled high up the nousts.

Gulls followed my ox and plough. The silent girl clapped her hands, for another furrow done.

We kept a bowl in a niche, to gather the coins for the voyage to Orkney.

My wife sold a hundred eggs to a sailor on the shore. The Dutchman gave her a shilling and a few herring.

A blackbird sat on the girl's forefinger, and sang and sang, for her alone it seemed.

Now there was a scattering of shillings in the bowl.

The dumb girl made the bowl sing and ring between her hands.

At her table my wife made fine round cheeses, and rounds of butter yellow as the moon.

All that work was for the pilgrimage.

In the month of June the sea trembled with blueness and light. The first of the barley was green in my rig.

My wife went here and there to the big houses, with knitted things and with eggs and cheese and butter.

When the blackbird sang to the daughter, 'What's all this stir and labour for? Why all the shillings?' the girl would laugh without sound and point south.

A wandering friar touched the girl's mouth, and went on.

The spinning wheel sang in the open door, morning to night. And my wife sang a song as the wheel turned.

The fishermen rowed home from the east with full baskets of silver fish. Boat after boat sailed in from the 'haaf' in the east.

All the women watched from the shore.

But the daughter was looking south.

August: month of the sickled corn.

The wife left her wheel and wool and bowl of shillings to glean corn in a score of crofts, first one, then another.

She of the locked mouth was often up at the chapel that month. She knelt by a lighted candle.

'A passage to Orkney?' said the skipper. 'In midwinter? Now, in the gray winds of September, is a good time for sailing. There will be storms in December, for sure. I can't guarantee you a passage at that dark time.'

The wife sold him a jersey for cold sea-nights.

'I could take you next week,' said the skipper, 'if this wind keeps.'

The girl shook her head. She counted twelve on her fingers: December.

Shillings lay in the bowl like a little heavy drift of snow.

I shut the ox and the two cows in the byre.

The girl filled the cruisie with oil and lit it, at sunset.

All were shadows in the croft, but for the shine on her soundless face.

In the month of souls, November, we visited the graves round the little church.

And I threshed oats in the barn after sunset.

The girl stood near the rock where the fishermen drowned six winters before. She wept without sound.

Darkness when we sailed from Shetland, in a still darkling sea.

Then the brief flame of noon.

Darkness when we came to Birsay, and were set ashore by the light of one lantern.

A feast of candles inside the kirk, seven red candles round the tomb of the martyr.

'It's good,' said the monk, 'that you have come this winter. Soon the bones of Saint Magnus are to be carried to Kirkwall.'

The dumb lass stayed by the tomb all night.

The monks sang, low and grave, in the choir.

Christus natus est, cried the girl at midnight.

Christ is born.

Christus natus est, sang the joyful monks.

Four Poems for Edwin Muir

1 FIFTEENTH OF MAY, 1887

A hundred Springs ago, the winter-byred
Beasts blundered at the sun
    And the fields of Folly
      Were littered with new lambs,

And a first sleepy bee began to bend
Marigold and mayflower for the barren
    Treasure of their cups,
      And the unyoked horse

Hurled out of servitude, a surge
Of hooves above the ocean thunders.
    Between equinox and solstice
      Torrents of boreal light,

The black ploughland a thin plash of green,
Scarecrow-kept. Now James Muir, farmer,
    Stands awkward beside his glebe, imagining
      Far on, the miracle of loaves.

I expect, somewhere in Orkney that day
A soul slipped down to a boat
    And the ebb bore a death into dawnlight . . .
      Tide turns now. See, the women —

Country welcomers round a wondering cry —
Are setting the new voyager in his crib.
    Far off, far off, against the headland
    Time surges, cries, celebrates.

2   *THE LOST CHILD*

They looked for him among the cornstalks.
He was not there.

In the field where the horses roamed
No sign of the child
Though one great plough-horse raised his head, listening.

Down at the shore
The limpet gatherers hadn't seen him.

'I think he'll be holding
An egg or a butterfly in his hand.'

He stoops to the bees and the clover.
A pure bead
Gathers, then falls forever through his thought.

I saw a boy chasing a small boy,
Their boots hidden
In little clouds of sun-dust.
The bronze of the school bell
Trembled around, like sword on shield.

That boy
Will trance a ship to the rim of the sea
Till his mother calls him.

Someone went in at the door of the green hill.
There the harp is,
Carved in stone among skulls and bronze helmets.
That rune will unlock
Time's labyrinth, door after door
To the tree and the apple.

3   *THE COAT*

In a croft door a boy puts on a coat
With a fish sewn on it
And a daffodil
And a great horse with a whirling hoof
And a quartered sun
And cornsheaves
And a high lonely hawk
And a seal on a rock —
The hem all stars and spindrift

The island women cover their heads on the shore

The boy in his coat of creatures, a Joseph
Journeys
Between the fifth and the sixth day

He lingers outside a tower

A gate opens. Seven iron masks
Consider the green coat.

4   CORMACK THE SAILOR

('My mother's name was Elizabeth Cormack . . . There is in Deerness
a ruined chapel which was built in the eighth or ninth century by an
Irish priest called Cormack the Sailor, who was later canonised . . .
Whether the names are connected over that great stretch of time in
that small corner no one can say; but it is conceivable, for in Orkney
families have lived in the same place for many hundreds of years,
and I like to think that some people in the parish, myself among
them, may have a saint among their ancestors, since some of the
Irish priests were not celibate'. Edwin Muir, *An Autobiography*.)

Listen to Cormac the sailor.
He is bent over a harp. He sings.

'When I see the cloud on the hill
I give praise to God.

When I see the sun on the many waters
The round ocean
And the quiet circle of the well
And in the rushing burn
I give praise to God.

I travelled in a ship from Ireland.
I stood in the warehouses
And discussed cargoes and bills-of-lading.
I entered houses
Where there was music, dancing, and verse.
Those things entranced me. Now
The lamp and the jar are lost in light,
I give praise to God.

In middle-Europe I woke from long sleep.
This harp stood at the wall.
Who left it there, an angel?
I give praise to God.

I have known praise and blame.
I have sat at the fire of a good woman
And have eaten her bread.
I have sat, darkling, in a place of bone.
I sailed back over the ocean.
Near a spring of clear water, my childhood,
Continually now *Laus Deo* I sing

When I hear thunder, or raindrops
I give praise to God.
I am an old man now, in a hood.
My fingers are twisted
And I have small taste for wine or fish
But more and more urgently
As days and months and seasons pass
As I see my skull in a stone that shines after rain
O clear and pure as larks in a blue morning
I sing, *Deo gratias.*

Autumn Equinox

If you say, 'I am light'
I answer, 'Darkness'.
If you say, 'I tended the rose bush'
I reply, 'Frost flowers'.
If you say, 'A girl is reading a letter with parted lips',
I see a widow on the roads.
She knocks at a door. She has candles and needles to sell.

'A bird carries a burning seed
Into the blizzard.'

'The loom of time
Casts, this sunset, the year's third coat, harvest'.

We are sisters of a golden king.
We have travelled
One from the pole, one from the burning wheel
To a tryst on a doorstep.
I will light the lamp now in the west window.
You set the sun, as always, broken flames on the hearth.
We bide together one night, gladly, in the House of Man.
We go again, at sunrise,
One to the ice, one to the cage of fire.

The Long Hall

The skald tuned his harp. The riff-raff
    Lounged between the barrel
    And the hearth (the Earl
        That winter night

Sat with the Bishop, a golden
    Cup between them, a loaf
    Tasting of honey, flames
        Eating the spitted ox).

Harp sang the swallowflight
    Through the lighted hall,
    A small troubling
        Between two dark doors.

Barnmen came in. Fishermen
    Shifted into the shadows.
    A kitchen girl carried
        A plate of bones

To the hungry hound. A keg
    Was broached. Outside
    Children went by, chanting
        Of snowflakes and apples.

Solstice

The winter tribute. It is time to go with the islands'
tribute

At the end of November
We set the keel for Norway, a lantern in the stern.
And had fair passage. And anchored in the fiord.
I knocked at the lodge of the castle.
A long gargoyle face — *The king is sick.*
A princess said, in the hall,
Winter will be long — there is no heir — What are we but
ice-maidens after today?
There entered the king's room soon
The seven with hoods over their faces.
Eat below with the horsemen. I was told.
'The treasurer?' The treasurer could not be lured from the hoard,
as if locked gold was the king's breath and blood.
A black bell shivered, once, in the tower.
The horsemen diced with blue fingers in the stable.
A girl put cinders in her hair.
The hooded seven
Stood round the last candle. One stooped in the chapel, holding
back his hood, in a rush of gray breath he quenched
the flame.

They went down,
They carried torches and the sword with runes on it, to a
ship.

The soul of the king will set out northwards, alone, at
$$\textit{midnight.}$$
Peasants and fishermen
Stood, red and black, at the edge of the circle of burning.
In the shadows, unmoving, the very poor.
The Orkney ship was five days out of the harbour.
Where should I leave
The gold and the poem and the jar I had carried from the
$$\text{west?}$$

They Came to an Inn

They came to an inn
   And they reined in the horses
Sat down with crusts and beer

They came to a river
   And they reined in the horses
A ferryman stood with a lantern

They came to a garden
   And they reined in the horses
A hand bled in a rosebush

They came to a smithy
   And they reined in the horses
Three nails and a long lance

They came to a mountain
   And they reined in the horses
Shepherds broke ice in the pass

They came to a palace
   And they reined in the horses
The eyes of the king were thorns

They came to a fair
    And they reined in the horses
They bargained for gold and a jar and a
                               web of silk

They came to a prison
    And they reined in the horses
The chains rang out like bells

They came to an island
    And they reined in the horses
Storm-watchers stood on the shore

And they came to a chapel

Epiphany Poem

The red king
  Came to a great water. He said,
    Here the journey ends.
    No keel or skipper on this shore.

The yellow king
  Halted under a hill. He said,
    Turn the camels round.
    Beyond, ice summits only.

The black king
  Knocked on a city gate. He said,
    All roads stop here.
    These are gravestones, no inn.

The three kings
  Met under a dry star.
    There, at midnight,
    The star began its singing.

The three kings
  Suffered salt, snow, skulls.
    They suffered the silence
    Before the first word.

The Twelve Days of Christmas:
Tinker Talk

I saw the four shepherds, black
In the sun's ruin.
Four star-cut shadows, soon.

Folk going to Kirkwall to pay the tax,
Cart after cart.
We trailed behind, packs clanging.

I stood awhile at the shore.
Three ships
Quested by needle and hidden star.

Fire on the quarry-stone rooted,
A winter rose.
Butterflies of snow everywhere, a gray whirl.

Our donkey danders
Up small roads
To poor crofts. We offer cheap enchantments.

We chew limpets. Their peat smoke
Cures the sea silver.
A scatter, struck gold, over barn floors.

The islands white whales in the snow.
The rook on the branch
Had black thorns in his throat.

I thought I heard a night cry, a bairn
Poorer than me.
A white dream, surely.

In the street of Kirkwall
Talk of troubles.
Soldiers in the slush, kestrel-headed.

I saw the shepherds. One
Folded a shivering lamb.
They lingered at the door of the inn.

The sun was a shuttered hovel
Last time we passed.
Look now, new bright roofbeams!

We took pans and mirrors to Hamnavoe.
Three foreign skippers,
The pier heaped with bonded cargoes.

Desert Rose

No one *will praise your beauty,* the poet said —
You must live and die alone.

Three travellers out of the morning rode.
They lingered. They stirred my incense. They
                                    journeyed on.

No shower or shade—
I suffered all day the barren gold of the sun.

A star lifted its head
And seemed to murmur to me alone,

All beyond time are made,
Star and poem, cornstalk and stone.

Now to the House-of-Bread
I guide three hungry gold-burdened men.

Midnight, the star throng, shed
Dew in my cup like wine.

Dance of the Months
A Christmas Card

January comes with his ice-crown.
February spilling thaw and snowdrops.
March, bursting loud cheeks!
Then April, with a troop of lambs and daffodils.
May, keeper of peat-hill and cuithe-stream.
June, covering the night fire in the north.
July, tall and blue as lupins.
August with the cut cornstalks.
September, dusting cobwebs from the lamp.
October, good witch, with apples and nuts.
November, host to shades and hallows.
December with snowflake and star.

In the inn of December, a fire,
A loaf, a bottle of wine.
Travellers, rich and poor, are on the roads.

The Last Gate

'Stop, travellers. The way goes no further.
Stop. Beyond this moor the tracks of wolf and of
        creatures that have no name.
Stop. Do you not hear the sea roaring under the
        broken cliff ledge?
I charge all travellers, that they should return
        to their lamps and flowers and cups.
No gold nor seal nor gun turns this sentry.
Stop. A few have gone into the blackness by other
        ways. No word of them has come
        back, ever.
Stop, friends. I stand before you in consideration
        of a duty owed between blood and
        stars: a sign of preservation.'

The keeper of the gate heard, coming on, the chatter
        and the hooves of a new company.

Then a word was proferred, a sign, at sunset.
The keeper unlatched the gate.
They went through with their creaking beasts, all three.

On one side, the burnt ocean.
On one, a desert of vitrified cities.
In front, a mountain with steps cut in the highest
        ice.

Far on, they saw what one took to be a star,
Or a man with a lantern,
The man who is sent out to guide travellers to an
        inn.

A Winter King

'Now,' said the sea king
'Freight the death ship
With jar and tapestry and gold.
I must sail alone, very far.
It is time for a new saga to be told.'

The king was bronze-bearded, not sick
                or meek-mouthed or old.
On the hull a bird had been cut,
Branch-beaked, a long gray wing.

Fishermen loosed the rope.
They sent the ship down the rollers
                with a darkling shout
Under the voyager's star.

Midnight Words

The red king said to the boy, 'You're too small
To shift such baggage.
Here, buy an apple or a bird.'

The yellow king said, 'Icicles
Hang like gray nails from the lintel, boy.'

The black king said, 'In my castle
The women would clothe you in blue silk.
Your cold face
Would be a star among the gold and ebony.'

The boy said, 'Here they come now,
The hill shepherds.
A rough lot. At midnight
They always come down for their jar of wine.'

The boy blew notes from his pipe.
Shepherds and kings followed the carol.

Carol: Kings and Shepherds

'Here's the place,' said the kings
   And the black one set on the sill a rose.

'At last, at last,' said the kings
   And the yellow one played, inside, his flute.

'Open the box', said the kings
   And the red one poured a torrent of gold.

   Then a troop of shepherds came.

The shepherd boy was cold as a root
And the old one like a thorn was cold
And the five shearers stood blue as ice.

   The shepherds brought to the place a winter lamb.

Christmas Poem

We are folded all
In a green fable
And we fare
From early
Plough-and-daffodil sun
Through a revel
Of wind-tossed oats and barley
Past sickle and flail
To harvest home,
The circles of bread and ale
At the long table.
It is told, the story—
We and earth and sun and corn are one.

Now kings and shepherds have come.
A wintered hovel
Hides a glory
Whiter than snowflake or silver or star.

A Winter Tale

In an island, no one escapes the sea.
Spume and gull everywhere.
The sea beats at the end of every road.

I think I will not stay long here.
'I am looking for this house' . . .
Across the boat
The ferryman shook his head at me.

Three old women mumbled
As if I had come
To burn the roofs over their heads.

A boy listened, above the waves' thunder and blaze.
His finger pointed
But drooped soon like a flower in a jam-jar.

The blacksmith
Had never heard of that house.
The beadle turned the pages of an old book
And shook his head.

The schoolmaster listened gravely.
The laird
Would not so much as open his door.

And the sea! Lamentation
Of sea at the North Head, in the darkness.
If the westerly slackens
It may be (said the ferryman) he will loosen
                                        the rope.

The innkeeper had one room,
Very expensive.
'We don't expect tourists at this time of
                                        year.'

By midnight, I had stood at every door
In the island but one,
And it a shelter for sheep.

House of Winter

At last, the house of winter. Find
On the sill
Intricate ice jewellery, a snowflake.

Open one dark door. Wind-flung,
A golden moth! Soon
A candle flame, tranquil and tall.

It is a bitter house. On the step
Birds starve.
The sign over the door is warped
    and faded.

Inside one chamber, see
A bare thorn.
Wait. A bud breaks. It is a white rose.

We think, in the heart of the house
A table is set
With a wine jar and broken bread.

The Child in the Snow

'Listen. Somewhere outside, a footfall' . . .
   A snowflake on the pane.

'I have heard it again, the low knocking' . . .
   The fall of a frozen bird.
   It is the sift of ash in the hearth.
   It is the sound a star makes on the
      longest night of the year, a silver harp-stroke.
   No one is out on a night like this.
   You heard a mouse between the walls,
   Or a lamb in the high fold, trembling.
   Turn over. Let your brain
   Brim with a winter hoard of dreams.

'At midnight I dreamed
Of a thin lost child in the snow.'

Snowman

Chime of ice chains between
Sky and freezing burn.
Swans on the loch are crystal
Sculptings.
Three children rend the new white
Flowing silk.
(Splinters of glass scatter from their mouths!)

In radiant tatters they robe
The Winter King.

Feast of Candles

Here a candle was set, for a cure on the hill
And there a candle, a shy flame, for a cradled
        one at the shore
And there now, a candle, swiftly set, the flame
        draught-flung: for a sailor in
        Ireland
A candle, laving pure flame on a face: and
        the mouth moved with a name and
        names, and a sorrow
Such a procession of flowers-of-flame, in winter
One by one, out of the bitter black night, under
        the stars
And an old woman, sifting names of else forgotten
        dead, with a bleak blown candle
And girls from the big farm, leaving their empty
        mirth outside, each girl a candle-
        bearer, and there children-brides-
        mothers-deathfolders-mourners
        (those five girls) beautifully
        lighted about the eyes and the
        hushed mouths
And after, a shepherd, shielding his flame, whispering
        'Saint Agnes'
Then fishermen from the boat *Fulmar,* each
        lighting his candle from the
        boat's lantern

And a candle set, as if the laird's face was
    kissed by an angel, the man's
    rock-hard face, and the mouth
    unlocked with a prayer
And another flame of candle that seemed to go
    out and gulped for life and
    folded wings like a summer
    butterfly: and that was the
    hen-wife and her candle
(And the monk gathered the folds of his cloak
    together at the altar and bent
    and prayed between two tall
    set-apart candles: in Latin
    whispers and a boy replied,
    hesitant with the Latin syllables,
    in country whispers)
And a flame set, and a flame set, and a flame
    set . . .
Then was the cry heard down at the shore
And there were whispers, 'The skipper'
For the ship *Olaf* would weigh that night for
    Trondheim, with news of Magnus
    and the light at his tomb beyond
    sun or stars or candles
Yet a dozen candles would be lit for that voyage,
    and brought from keel to kirk, for
    a blessing on the voyage
And there again a candle set, Bjorn the ploughman
    seeking good furrows to follow his
    oxen and plough

And a candle set, the flame borne by the earl's
        poet purer than words he would ever
        strike, but he had no sorrow for that:
        who shall say whom wax-and-
        wick-and-petal was set there for, a
        lady or a light to welcome the spring,
        or a drop to be lost in the ocean of
        the first and last Light
Then two children from the hill, one crying for his
        candle was out, but the other rekindled
        it, and the tallow rooted in warm
        dribblings
(And the altar-boy turned a page for the priest)
And a wave of lights, with sea breath, broke
        upon the door. And that was
        the sailors . . .
Then the priest, in the stone ship, turned and
        blessed that feast of candles on
        Candlemas night.

The Gardener: Easter

1

Now it's Spring, there's not that much to do.
Daffodils open, then tulips
(The roses very doubtful this year.)
The blackbirds open their throats.
The masons have finished the tomb, and gone away.

2

Soldiers go past, a bronze column.
Trouble in the city.
Always trouble, in street and hill, these days.
The quietest place is my garden.

3

I worry about the rosebush.
Has the worm gotten in?
The worm eats the coat of white roses, often,
To a rigging of rags, a scarecrow.
Ten summers ago, it all but died.

4

Nightingales sang all last night.
I hardly slept.
Joseph came with my wages, a silver piece, in the morning.
Then a rout of children
Pleading, at noon, for olive leaves.

5

Crowds going past, surging, lingering, herded by soldiers,
Among them one,
A young man carrying his tree of death.
(I dare not look at that.
I nip the tainted buds from the rosebush.)

6

Joseph at my door at sunset. *Hurry, man!*
Bring jars of oil. Bring
A web of linen.
It is not my business
Who is to be the guest in the hollow rock.

7

A woman crying beside the fountain.
The last stars.
Two of those fishermen, I think,
Hesitant at the gate, watchful.
I should send those folk about their business.
A dove furls in my dead tree
At gray of dawn.
And now the tree is clusters of light and incense!

The Flute in the Garden
(to Judith)

January

    The flute sang
    Silently
    in the ear of a snowman

February

    A little white blossom
    unfurled
    through a stop in the flute

March

    The flute
    was washed in a wave of new green grass

April

    A daffodil danced in the wind, a splash of sun
    over
    the sleeping flute

May

    Small lyrics
    — daisy, buttercup, clover —
    covered the mouth of the flute

June

    Blackbird cocked a head at the flute, then

    trilled, questioned

July

    In the rosebush over

    the flute

    roses whirled, a white ballet

August

    A honeybee

    blundered across the silent flute

    — sweetness!

September

    Fall light, leaves,

    on

    Orpheus asleep in those chambers

October

    Waken the flute with a gift of apples,

    girl

November

    Can the flute

    follow her in to the fires and the lamp?

December

    Flute-song,

    star in the solstice tree